# Dealing with Dawkins

## John Blanchard

**EP BOOKS**

1st Floor Venture House, 6 Silver Court, Watchmead,
Welwyn Garden City, UK, AL7 1TS

web: http://www.epbooks.org
e-mail: sales@epbooks.org

EP Books are distributed in the USA by:
JPL Distribution
3741 Linden Avenue Southeast
Grand Rapids, MI 49548
E-mail: orders@jpldistribution.com
Tel: 877.683.6935

**British Library Cataloguing in Publication Data available**

ISBN 978–1–78397–146–6

# Contents

# 1

# **The man and the mission**

Clinton Richard Dawkins was born in Nairobi, Kenya, in 1941 and had what he has called 'a harmless Anglican upbringing'. As a nine-year-old he had 'brief periods of doubt' about God's existence, triggered by realizing that there were so many different religions, but recovered belief in God when persuaded by the argument from design. He joined the Church of England and for some time carried 'a guttering torch' for it,[1] but when he 'discovered Darwinism' as a teenager, 'the last vestige of religious faith disappeared for ever'.[2]

After attending Oundle School, Northamptonshire, he read zoology at Balliol College, Oxford, graduating in 1962, then did further research at Oxford, leading to his doctoral thesis, *Selective Pecking in the Domestic Chick*. After several years on the faculty of the University of California at Berkeley he returned to lecture at Oxford, where he was later appointed the first Charles Simonyi

Professor for the Public Understanding of Science, a position he held until his retirement in 2008.

He first hit the headlines in 1976 with his book *The Selfish Gene*, in which he emphasized the part played by genetics in the theory of evolution and argued that 'we, like all other animals, are machines created by our genes'.[3] In the same book he invented the word 'meme' in referring to a 'cultural replicator' that passes on to other people such things as tunes, ideas, fashions and phrases, and even belief in God. In *The Blind Watchmaker* (1986) he denied that the complexity we see in nature points to a supernatural creator. In *Climbing Mount Improbable* (1996) he argued that evolution produces amazing results not by sudden massive leaps but by countless tiny changes over millions of years. In *Unweaving the Rainbow* (1998) he claimed that science alone is the key to understanding beauty and wonder in the universe.

These and other titles sold well, but they all took a back seat when *The God Delusion* was published in 2006. His earlier books 'did not set out to convert anyone',[4] but in the preface to *The God Delusion* he made his intentions clear: 'If this book works as I intend, religious readers who open it will be atheists when they put it down.'[5] Later in the book he identified his target: 'I am attacking God, all gods, anything and everything supernatural, wherever and whenever they have been or will be invented.'[6]

*The God Delusion* has been praised by many reviewers and criticized by many others, including some who share Dawkins' world-view. Professor Michael Ruse, of Florida State University, went so far as to write, '*The God Delusion* makes me ashamed to be an atheist.'[7] A number of excellent books have been written in response to it[8] and others may follow, but there is also a need for a brief, simply written response that exposes Dawkins' mindset and pinpoints some of the major flaws in his case against God. It would have to avoid complicated or technical language whenever possible and present the case for God in a way that could easily be understood by those who might not be willing to wade through a longer volume. I believe this small book ticks all those boxes.

In challenging an opponent's views it is easy to overstep the mark and in the heat of the moment attack the person rather than his or her principles, theories or ideas. There is no excuse for this when writing, as the text can be carefully reviewed and revised before being released, and I will make sure that in this publication I 'play the ball, not the man'. Although Dawkins is one of today's most vocal atheists, I have no reason for attacking him as a person. For all I know he may well be caring and compassionate to those in need, give generously to charitable causes, be a thoughtful and supportive husband and an ideal person to have as a next-door neighbour, so this book will just address his ideas and beliefs. I could have called it *Countering the philosophy* and theories of Richard Dawkins, with particular regard to the relationship between religion, Christianity and the natural sciences, but that hardly trips off the tongue. *Dealing with Dawkins* will do—and I believe he will not object to it as, after hearing a presentation by the British apologist Paul Taylor on 'Deconstructing Dawkins', he assured the speaker that he had no problem with that title.

This small volume will obviously not be able to examine in detail any of the major issues raised in *The God Delusion* (on which it will concentrate) or engage at length with his later title, *The Greatest Show on Earth* (2009), in which he claims to lay out the evidence for evolution. Instead, it will look briefly at eight key issues around which Dawkins builds his case against God. If it works as I intend, those who doubt or deny God's existence will see that Dawkins' atheist ideas are fundamentally flawed.

Woodrow Wilson, the twenty-eighth President of the United States, once joked, 'I not only use all the brains that I have, but all I can borrow.' For obvious reasons I will do a lot of borrowing.

# 2

# Science:
# the answer to everything?

When William Temple was Archbishop of Canterbury (1942–1944) he admitted, 'My ignorance of science is so profound as to be distinguished,'[1] and at least on that score I am on a par with an archbishop. This hardly qualifies me to tangle with Richard Dawkins, who earned a degree in science at Oxford University and has numerous honorary degrees and awards for his writing on scientific subjects. Scientifically speaking we are a laughable mismatch, yet there are issues on which he can be challenged.

To begin with, Dawkins claims, 'Religion is no longer a serious candidate in the field of explanation. It is completely superseded by science.'[2] Yet *this is not a scientific statement*, but merely the opinion of someone whose understanding of religion falls far short of his scientific expertise. In medieval times 'science' meant all knowledge. Now, 'no generally accepted definition of what science is is agreed on by a majority of philosophers of science,'[3] but the following will be an adequate guideline: *Science is the ongoing process of discovering truth about the natural world.*

True science is not certainty, but the search *for* certainty. It is inquisitive, honest and self-correcting, prepared to amend or replace statements it once claimed to be true. Nobel Prize-winning physicist Richard Feynman often maintained, 'Scientific knowledge is a body of statements of varying degrees of uncertainty— some unsure, some nearly sure, but none absolutely certain.'[4] In 2009, Lord Rees, President of the Royal Society, went so far as to say, 'Ultimately, the history of science is a history of best guesses,'[5] while in the same year Richard Dawkins told BBC radio listeners, 'Science often makes progress by correcting its mistakes.'[6]

None of this is to criticize science or reject scientific theories that have proved reliable, but it shows that science has limitations. Relying as it must on observation and experiment, there are things that cannot be explored or explained by the scientific method. We will come to Dawkins' views about God later, but for the moment will focus on how he smuggles in the idea that science can tell us everything. On the BBC television programme *Soul of Britain*, he declared, 'I think science really has fulfilled the need that religion did in the past, of explaining things, explaining why we are here, what is the origin of life, where did the world come from, what life is all about … *science has the answers.*[7] The words I have emphasized would make religion irrelevant and science supreme, yet all four claims can easily be dismissed.

## Science cannot explain why we are here

Over the centuries, countless ideas have been put forward to explain human existence, many of them bizarre. Dawkins claims that, while religion is unable to point us in the right direction, science can unravel the mystery. Yet he fails to explain this and is flatly contradicted by another passionate atheist, Steve Jones, Professor of Genetics at University College London: 'Science cannot answer the questions that philosophers—or children— ask: why are we here, what is the point of being alive, how ought we to behave? … These questions may be interesting, but scientists are no more qualified to comment on them than is anyone else.'[8] Jones is right, and Dawkins' claim is an empty sound bite.

## Science cannot explain the origin of life

Dawkins endorses Charles Darwin's idea of evolution by natural selection over millions of years, with the fittest specimens of species surviving and gradually leading to more complex forms of life. Evolution's so-called 'tree of life' covers all living things that have ever existed on our planet, from the first life form to humankind; as

Dawkins puts it, 'We are all descended from what might have been something like bacteria.'[9] He is so sure of this that he adds, 'It is absolutely safe to say that if you meet somebody who claims not to believe in evolution, that person is ignorant, stupid or insane (or wicked, but I'd rather not consider that).'[10]

This kind of statement is frequently made by atheists, *but it fails to explain how life began.* Before evolution can begin there has to be something capable of evolving; before natural selection gets under way there has to be something to select. Dawkins admits that natural selection 'needs some luck to get started'[11] and that the emergence of self-replicating life forms out of nothing is 'exceedingly improbable'.[12] He then sidesteps the problem by suggesting that 'given time, anything is possible',[13] but as there is no way of proving this he is confusing guesswork with fact.

Darwin knew nothing about DNA, an amazing molecule packed with a staggering amount of genetic information arranged in a highly organized code, or language, that allows all living things to function, grow and reproduce. More information is housed in the DNA of each one of the trillions of cells in a human body than in the entire *Encyclopaedia Britannica*. If the *Encyclopaedia Britannica* dropped out of the sky in computer code it would be accepted without question that there must be extra-terrestrial intelligence.

Then surely the information in DNA must have an intelligent source? *Where did this information come from?* Information theory expert Professor Werner Gitt quotes this conclusion of a conference on the origin of life: 'There is no known natural law through which matter can give rise to information, neither is there any physical process or material phenomenon known that can do this.'[14] To claim that science can explain the origin of life is to confuse fantasy with fact and in 2009 Dawkins contradicted his own claim by admitting, 'We don't know how life itself began.'[15] The Austrian theoretical physicist Wolfgang Pauli, winner of the 1945 Nobel Prize for Physics, put it perfectly: 'All scientific methods fail when questions of origins are involved.'[16]

## Science cannot explain where the world came from

The Big Bang theory says that the entire universe came into being some fourteen billion years ago, but for all the claims made on its behalf it raises a lot of questions. How could a random explosion produce the elegant and dependable laws of nature that govern it? The British mathematical physicist Sir Roger Penrose has put the odds against this happening by chance at one in $10^{10^{123}}$ —a number so vast that it is said to have more zeros than the total number of particles in the entire universe. Could we also put this down to 'luck'? What exactly was it that went 'Bang!'? Where did the necessary energy and matter come from? Did anything exist before time, space and matter? How did the laws of nature come about? *Why is there something rather than nothing?* As the distinguished British physicist Stephen Hawking admits, 'Science … cannot answer the question: why does the universe bother to exist? I don't know the answer to that.'[17] Science cannot tell us why things are the way they are, but the contemporary American pastor Timothy Keller says, 'The theory that there is a God who made the world accounts for the evidence we see better than the theory that there is no God.'[18] The American astrophysicist Arno Penzias, who shared the 1978 Nobel Prize for Physics, adds this interesting comment: 'The best data we have are exactly what I would have predicted had I nothing to go on but the five books of Moses, the Psalms, the Bible as a whole.'[19]

## Science cannot explain what life is all about

Richard Feynman has been called 'the Great Explainer', yet admits. 'Through all ages, men have tried to fathom the meaning of life … If we take everything into account … then I think we must frankly admit that *we do not know*' (emphasis added).[20] As we have seen, Dawkins claims that science has the answer, though when asked about the purpose of life in a 1995 issue of *The Observer*, he replied, 'Well, there is no purpose, and to ask what it is is a silly question. It has the same status as "What is the colour of jealousy?"'[21] This does seem like trying to have it both ways—claiming science can answer the question, but also saying that the question is silly and should not even be asked.

The closest Dawkins gets to offering what might be called a 'purpose' for human life is the core message of one of his books: 'We are survival machines—robot vehicles blindly programmed to preserve the selfish molecules known as genes.'[22] Elsewhere he added, 'Living organisms exist for the benefit of DNA rather than the other way round.'[23] Yet our lives deny that we are machines; our feelings, our hopes, our longings, our fears, our desires, our likes and dislikes, our choices and decisions all shout that we are *not* robots. Unlike robots, we are conscious and know that we are conscious. We also know that we are responsible for our actions, but if our genes determine our behaviour, have we no option but to do what they dictate? Are we not free to make moral choices? If not, how can we praise virtue and condemn vice? Why should we ever feel guilty or ashamed? How can we operate a judicial system if the rapist, the child abuser and the murderer can claim they were only dancing to the music of their genes? As journalist Janet Daley says, 'The idea of putting anyone on trial for anything at all becomes absurd.'[24]

Dawkins goes on to say that although we are robots programmed by our selfish genes, 'If we understand what our genes are up to ... we may then at least have the chance to upset their designs.'[25] But how can robots rebel? In his book *There is a God* the British philosopher Antony Flew, previously rated the world's most notorious atheist, examined Dawkins' claim that we are merely machines created by our genes and came to this conclusion: 'None of it is true—or even faintly sensible.'[26]

## History or his story?

In his latest book, *The Greatest Show on Earth*, Dawkins concentrates on evolution. He says it is 'not intended as an anti-religious book', but by adding, 'I've done that, it's another T-shirt, this is not the place to wear it again,'[27] he tells us that he had written God out of the script before he starts.

His main weapon for eliminating God is to call all who disagree with his view on evolution 'history-deniers', on a par with students irritating their history teacher by insisting 'that the Romans never existed'.[28] More seriously, he likens them to those who deny that the Holocaust ever happened. Amazingly, he even claims that the evidence for evolution is '*at least as strong* as the evidence for the Holocaust, *even allowing for eyewitnesses to the Holocaust*' (emphasis added).[29] The rhetoric lasts to the end of the book: rejecting evolution 'is equivalent to believing that the width of North America is less than 10 yards,'[30] and 'history-deniers' are like people 'who believe it takes one month for the Earth to go around the sun'.[31] This may be entertaining to some, but once again it contributes nothing to the discussion.

The first chapter reveals Dawkins' mindset. In discussing theories he accurately confirms the dictionary distinction between a hypothesis that has been 'confirmed or established by observation or experiment', and 'a mere hypothesis, speculation, conjecture'.[32] He then explains that when in mathematics the evidence in favour of a theory is overwhelming and there has never been a successful attempt to dislodge it, it becomes a 'theorem'. In Dawkins' view evolution is a theorem, but to draw a distinction between his scientific claim and one that is purely mathematical he invents a new word and calls it a 'theorum'. He admits that a scientific 'theorum' cannot be proved in the same way as a mathematical theorem, but claims that 'common sense treats it as a fact in the same sense as the "theory" that the Earth is round and not flat is a fact, and the theory that green plants obtain energy from the sun is a fact'.[33] A few pages earlier he uses the same trick by stating, 'Evolution is a fact in the same sense as it is a fact that Paris is in the Northern Hemisphere.'[34] On BBC Television he directly dismissed all who disagreed: 'Those who believe in creation are deluded to the point of perversity.'[35]

In pressing home his contention, Dawkins is not averse to being economical with the truth. To claim that all bishops and theologians who have paid attention to the evidence—except those 'woefully uninformed'— 'have given up the struggle against it'[36] is simply not true. To state that 'educated priests and professors of theology' have 'no problem with evolution'[37] deviously infers that there are no exceptions. To say of evolution, 'No reputable scientist disputes it'[38] contradicts the fact that countless highly qualified scientists do. For example, more than 800 scientists with PhD degrees recently signed a public statement that reads, 'We are sceptical of claims for the ability of random mutation and natural selection to account for the complexity of life.'[39] To add the arrogant claim, 'No unbiased reader will close the book doubting it'[40] takes him into the realm of prophecy, where he should not be taken seriously.

Dawkins maintains, 'It is the plain truth that we are cousins of chimpanzees, somewhat more distant cousins of monkeys, more distant cousins still of aardvarks and manatees, yet more distant cousins of bananas and turnips …',[41] and ends chapter 1 by claiming, 'The facts of evolution are far more numerous, more convincing, more incontrovertible, than any other eyewitness reports that have ever been used, in any court of law, in any century, to establish guilt in any crime.'[42] In *The Blind Watchmaker* he makes it clear that nothing will convince him otherwise: 'Even if there were no actual evidence in favour of Darwinism (there is, of course) we should still be justified in preferring it over all rival theories.'[43] His story can be summarized like this: 'There is no God; science has all the answers; evolution is proven beyond all doubt.'

Case closed? Not quite! In response to a question put to him by The Edge Foundation at the end of 2005 he replied, 'I believe that all life, all intelligence, all creativity and all "design" anywhere in the universe is the direct or indirect product of Darwinian natural selection.' However, what makes his reply both interesting and revealing is the question to which he was responding: 'What do you believe is true *even though you cannot prove it?*'

The rider is significant. To claim that science can explain everything, and in the process eliminate God, is not a statement of fact, but a leap of blind faith because, properly understood, science points us beyond its own limits. In an open review letter, the contemporary author and pastor David Robertson told Dawkins, 'Your view, that the universe is only physical, is a hypothesis and one that is largely based on wishful thinking. In fact, your position is a kind of "science of the gaps".'[44] The US National Academy of Science underlines this: 'Science is a way of knowing about the natural world. It is limited to explaining the natural world through natural causes. Science can say nothing about the supernatural. Whether God exists or not is a question about which science is neutral.'[45] Francis Collins, the distinguished geneticist best known for his leading role in the Human Genome Project, agrees: 'There is no conflict in being a rigorous scientist and a person who believes in a God who takes a personal interest in each one of us. Science's domain is to explore nature. God's domain is the spiritual world, a realm not possible to explore with the tools and language of science.'[46]

All of this is confirmed by a well-known atheist who has written extensively on the subject and says, 'Science has no way to disprove the existence of a supreme being'.[47] His name? Richard Dawkins.

# 3

# Morality:

# rights and wrongs

In the preface to *The God Delusion* Dawkins asks, 'Don't we need God, in order to be good?', then adds, 'Please read Chapters 6 and 7 to see why this is not so.'[1] Chapter 6 has the surprising title, 'The roots of morality: why are we good?' and suggests four reasons why evolution could account for human goodness. Firstly, our 'selfish' genes programme us to help those within our own social group; secondly, 'reciprocal altruism' ('You scratch my back and I'll scratch yours'); thirdly, a yearning to earn a good reputation for kindness and generosity; and, fourthly (though he is not certain about this), the wish to demonstrate a measure of dominance or superiority.

He offers no convincing evidence for these interesting ideas, which need to be read alongside something he said elsewhere: 'We get our immorality largely from our Darwinian past. [From it] we get our selfishness, we get our drive for self-interest, for ruthlessness, for cruelty perhaps, and I think the first thing we should do is throw out Darwinism; we should regard Darwin's natural selection as a great evil ... Although, of course, we remain Darwinian as far as our understanding of how the world got to be the way it is.'[2] Some years earlier he admitted, 'Universal love and the welfare of the species as a whole are concepts that simply do not make evolutionary sense.'[3]

Elsewhere he adds a rider: 'We are built as gene machines and cultured as meme machines, but we have the power to turn against our creators. We, alone on earth, can rebel against the tyranny of our selfish replicators.'[4] He qualifies this by suggesting that our instinct to do good things might be 'misfirings' in the course of evolution, what he calls 'blessed, precious mistakes.'[5] Anyone who thinks Dawkins' statements are confusing will understand why Kathleen Jones, Professor of Social Policy in the University of York, says they form 'a tortuous argument':

First, he insists on the existence of a ruthless and overriding life principle; then he asserts that it includes some form of 'Darwinian' morality; then he recognizes that this is not a sufficient explanation for altruism, and says that altruism is the result of 'mistakes' in which the selfish gene is really acting against its own interests. Finally, he says that he is thankful for the mistakes![6]

Chapter 7 of *The God Delusion* has the title, 'The "Good" Book and the changing moral *Zeitgeist*' (a German word meaning 'the spirit of the age'). Dawkins tries to destroy the Bible's 'goodness' by pinpointing horrific things done in the Old Testament (sometimes, he alleges, by God),[7] but though his racy language may amuse some of his fellow atheists it generates more heat than light. His thinking seems to go like this: 'These people believed in God; they did evil things; God was sometimes actively implicated; surely such a God does not exist.' (Dawkins calls him 'an appalling role model' and an 'evil monster'.)[8] In all of this, Dawkins ignores a fundamental fact: *the accounts concerned were recording events, not setting us examples of how to behave.*

He also ignores the Bible's teaching about the holiness of God and the sinfulness of man. He calls the well-known story of Noah's ark 'charming'[9] but the moral of the story 'appalling'[10] and summarizes it like this: 'God took a dim view of humans, so he (with the exception of one family) drowned the lot of them.'[11] This seems to turn God into an ogre—but does it? The Bible records that God, who is 'majestic in holiness' (Exodus 15:11), created man and placed him in a perfect environment, pouring out on him an uninterrupted flow of blessing. But man rebelled against his Maker and degenerated into such vile behaviour that 'every intention of the thoughts of his heart was only evil continually' (Genesis 6:5). Yet there was at least one exception: 'Noah found favour in the eyes of the Lord' (Genesis 6:8), who used him to offer forgiveness to all who would turn from their sin (see 2 Peter 2:5). It was only when Noah's contemporaries persistently rejected God's gracious offer that catastrophic judgement fell on them. To get to his punchline Dawkins ignores all of this and asks, 'Why should a divine being, with creation and eternity on his mind, care a fig for petty human malefactions?'[12] This betrays his ignorance of the holiness of God, the sinfulness of man, the nature of sin and God's unfailing concern for his fallen creation.

As to the 'changing moral *zeitgeist*', many will question Dawkins' claim that over the centuries moral and ethical standards have surged upwards in an 'advancing wave' and that in spite of 'local and temporary setbacks … the progressive trend is unmistakable and it will continue'.[13] As the twentieth century dawned many longed for a global utopia but the dream soon died, with over 75,000,000 slaughtered in two world wars. Soon afterwards, atheistic Communism swept around the world and more than doubled that number of victims in the People's Republic of China, the Soviet Union, Cambodia, North Korea, Africa, Afghanistan, Vietnam, Eastern Europe and elsewhere. Were these 'local and temporary setbacks'? What about today's repressive regimes and countries where crime rates and a spirit of lawlessness are staining the culture? Is racism disappearing? Is there less injustice? Is materialism on the way out? Is our generation becoming more honest, selfless, generous and humble? Many would suggest that any trend in the *zeitgeist* is not upward.

Dawkins rightly champions human rights and concern for personal dignity, yet science is unable to answer his crucial question: 'How, then, do we decide what is right and what is wrong?'[14] As John Lennox, Professor of Mathematics at the University of Oxford, loves to illustrate, 'Science can tell you that if you add strychnine to someone's drink it will kill them. But science cannot tell you whether it is morally right or wrong to put strychnine into your grandmother's tea so that you can get your hands on her property.'[15]

Dawkins admits, 'I don't know on the whole what is moral,'[16] and that 'Science has no methods for deciding what is ethical,'[17] but he is sure that any general consensus about right and wrong 'has no obvious connection with religion'.[18] We certainly cannot take morality from man-made religious systems, all of which are flawed and many of which have decidedly questionable moral codes, but Christianity stands apart. Dawkins fails to see this. He rightly commends racial equality, then states that 'a common humanity with members of other races and with the other sex' are 'both deeply unbiblical ideas'.[19]

This flatly contradicts the Bible's teaching that God 'made from one man every nation of mankind to live on all the face of the earth' (Acts 17:26) and ignores the fact that, as Kathleen Jones puts it, the New Testament Gospels lie behind 'the growing opposition to racism, sexism, ageism, disablism and all the other isms'.[20]

The Bible's teaching underlines the fundamental fact that man's ultimate rights are not determined by custom or consensus, but lie in his unique creation 'in the image of God' (Genesis 1:27). As Kathleen Jones rightly claims, 'Only Christianity tells us what fingerprinting suggested and DNA confirms: that each of us—all the untold millions of human beings right through the ages—*is unique and valuable*' (emphasis added).[21]

## The compass

When we face moral choices our awareness of moral law is triggered by the conscience, but where does this moral compass get its authority? There would seem to be just four possibilities.

The first is that it springs from *nature*, but this is obviously not the case. Admitting, 'I do have a strongly developed sense of good', Dawkins adds, 'But as a biologist I haven't a very well worked-out story where that comes from … I would … say that it is just something that has emerged.'[22] Yet evolution cannot account for moral values; it is impossible to jump from atoms to ethics and from molecules to morality. As the world-famous author C. S. Lewis argues, 'If we are to make moral judgements ... then we must believe that *the conscience is not a product of Nature*. It can be valid only if it is an offshoot of some absolute moral wisdom, a wisdom which exists absolutely "on its own" and is not a product of non-moral, non-rational Nature' (emphasis added).[23]

The second possibility is that we *ourselves* are the source of moral authority, yet this idea implodes, as we each have our own ideas as to what is right or wrong. The American author Ernest Hemingway said, 'What is moral is what you feel good after, and what is immoral is what you feel bad after,'[24] but this puts moral choices on a par with selecting items from a restaurant menu—Beef or chicken? Tea or coffee? Nobody in their right mind could sign up to this approach, which would amount to a moral free-for-all when nobody could blame anybody for anything.

The third possibility is that conscience has its moral base in *culture*, the general flow of public opinion, yet this idea is also fatally flawed. Why should public opinion be any better than private opinion? On what basis can one culture judge another to be right or wrong? What happens when cultures move the goalposts, allowing things they once said were wrong and outlawing things they once said were right? In some cultures people respect their neighbours; in some, they are allowed to eat them; in others, 'honour killings' among family members are acceptable; can they all be right?

The only other alternative is that conscience is best explained by *an objective moral law* that lies outside of nature, personal choice and the prevailing culture. Without this, conscience has no traction and we are left hopelessly adrift, with no objective moral values and no way of defining right and wrong. As Edgar Andrews says, 'We can only distinguish good morality from bad morality by appealing to some independent standard.'[25] Even an outspoken atheist such as the Australian philosopher J. L. Mackie grasped something of this: 'Moral properties ... are most unlikely to have arisen in the ordinary course of events without an all-powerful god to create them.'[26]

The solution would be a perfect, unchangeable and personal lawgiver, and the God revealed in the Bible is precisely that. In a world without such a God we would be morally bankrupt and blind. As 'The law of the Lord is perfect' (Psalm 19:7) and he is unchangeable (see Malachi 3:6), God's character shows why absolute moral values are as they are. As the contemporary American author Jay Wegter maintains, 'Who God is and what he has said infallibly determines what is real, what is true, what is right and what is wrong.'[27] Our creation by God explains not only why we sense ourselves to be hard-wired to believe in right and wrong and to know which is better, but why temptation, guilt and shame are inescapable parts of human experience. Even of those who deny his existence, the Bible says that the law of God 'is written on their hearts' (Romans 2:15).

After questioning why euthanasia, homosexual behaviour or abortion should be condemned, Dawkins writes, 'Fortunately, however, morals do not have to be absolute.'[28] He offers no proof for this, which is hardly surprising, as the idea self-destructs. The claim makes a moral statement, but *if morals do not have to be absolute, we cannot be absolutely sure that the statement is absolutely true.*

In their book *Answering the New Atheism*, university professors Scott Hahn and Benjamin Wiker say, 'Once we brush away surface similarities, we discover that *in principle* Christians and atheists inhabit different moral universes.'[29] They are right. In a godless world what one animal does to another is morally irrelevant; mass murder has the same moral significance as brushing dandruff off one's collar. Dawkins would seem to agree: 'The universe we observe has precisely the properties we should expect if there is at bottom no design, no purpose, *no evil and no good*. Nothing but blind, pitiless indifference. DNA neither knows nor cares. DNA just is, and we dance to its music' (emphasis added).[30]

Can we live with this? When I was addressing a meeting in Oxford an atheist shouted at me, 'Morality is relative', yet less than twenty-four hours earlier a Korean student at Virginia Polytechnic Institute and State University had killed thirty-two people and wounded twenty-five others in the deadliest shooting incident by a single gunman in United States history. Was what he did relatively evil or absolutely evil? Was he merely dancing to the music of his genes?

In 2006, Francis Collins pointed to a more sensible alternative: 'After twenty-eight years as a believer, the Moral Law still stands out for me as the strongest signpost to God. More than that, it points to a God who cares about human beings, and a God who is infinitely good and holy.'[31]

# Religion:
# the root of all evil?

Alister McGrath, Professor of Historical Theology at Oxford University (and a one-time atheist) is not exaggerating when he says that 'Religion to Dawkins is like a red rag to a bull.'[1] Dawkins agrees with the American physicist Steven Weinberg that 'Religion is an insult to human dignity,'[2] and sees all religion as 'very largely an enemy of truth'.[3] Elsewhere he calls the idea that there is one God 'the great unmentionable evil at the centre of our culture'.[4] This is similar to a comment by another well-known atheist, Christopher Hitchens, who claims, 'Religion poisons everything.'[5]

Claiming that religion is a major root of great evil, Dawkins echoes the theme of John Lennon's song 'Imagine' and at the beginning of *The God Delusion* writes:

Imagine no suicide bombers, no 9/11, no 7/7, no Crusades, no witch-hunts, no Gunpowder Plot, no Indian partition, no Israeli/Palestinian wars, no Serb/Croatian/ Muslim massacres, no persecution of Jews as 'Christ-killers', no Northern Ireland 'troubles', no 'honour killings', no shiny-suited bouffant-haired televangelists fleecing gullible people of their money ('God wants you to give till it hurts'). Imagine no Taliban to blow up ancient statues, no public beheadings of blasphemers, no flogging of female skin for the crime of showing an inch of it.[6]

I share his outrage at the violence and other evil things done in the name of religion, yet he overstates his case, as in several of his examples religion was not the trigger. (He later accepts that the Northern Ireland 'troubles', when some 3,000 people lost their lives, were essentially political rather than religious.)[7] He builds his case by ignoring the overwhelming majority of religious believers and concentrating almost entirely on extremists of one kind or another. He did the same in his 2006 BBC television series *The Root of all Evil?* when arguing that humanity would be better off without any religion. This may explain why a senior atheist scientist at Oxford University called the series 'pseudo-intellectual drivel'.[8]

Hideous evil has been done in the name of religion. As a Christian I cannot defend some of the things done in the name of Christianity, such as the Crusades against Muslims and others in the Middle East and elsewhere

(1095–1291) and the notorious Inquisitions between 1478 and 1870 in Spain, Portugal and Italy. Modern examples include the People's Temple, founded by Jim Jones in 1955 and leading to 900 of its members committing suicide in 1978, and the Branch Davidian Seventh-Day Adventist cult, under the leadership of David Koresh, which was wiped out following a siege at its headquarters outside Waco, Texas, in 1993. Yet genuine Christianity cannot possibly be blamed for these as their leaders were not following Christ's teaching. To blame Christianity for all the evil done in its name is to play fast and loose with the facts. Evil things done in the name of Christianity do not settle the question of its integrity. Counterfeit Christianity no more proves that the real thing cannot be trusted than forged currency means that we should reject the genuine article. From time to time viciously evil things have been done in the name of Christ, but never in the spirit of Christ. There are places in the world today where children and young people are trained to become terrorists in the name of religion, but nowhere is this being done by those who are true followers of Jesus Christ.

Following his 'Imagine' theme, Dawkins hints that in an atheist world people would not bulldoze religious buildings or destroy religious icons,[9] yet this ignores the fact that more brutality has been carried out by atheists than by those acting in the name of religion. It is a fact of history that millions were slaughtered as Communism, driven by atheism, swept across Europe and elsewhere. Lenin believed that killing Christians was a social obligation and stated, 'Every religious idea, every idea of God, every flirtation with the idea of God is unutterable vileness.'[10]

Nazism's driving philosophy was neither Christian nor religious, though it is almost impossible to penetrate Hitler's thinking. Raised in the Roman Catholic Church, he littered his speeches with references to God and Jesus and with quotations from the Bible. In a 1922 speech he even referred to Jesus as 'my Lord and Saviour',[11] yet in 1941 labelled Christianity 'the heaviest blow that ever struck humanity'.[12] German soldiers may have had 'Gott mitt uns' (God with us) on their belt buckles as they ravaged Europe, but this 'God' was one of Hitler's own invention. His murderous Holocaust, which slaughtered six million Jews, was diametrically opposed to Christian teaching and was linked to his belief that Darwin's ideas about the survival of the fittest meant human beings were disposable.

Atheist world-views drove Mao Tse-Tung to kill millions of his fellow countrymen in China and the Communist dictator Pol Pot to eliminate some twenty per cent of Cambodia's population in the notorious 'killing fields'. For Dawkins to claim, 'Individual atheists may do evil things, but they don't do evil things in the name of atheism,'[13] is naïve. A modern scholar has estimated that deaths caused by so-called Christian rulers over a five-hundred-year period amount to only one per cent of the deaths caused by Stalin, Hitler and Mao Tse-Tung in the course of a few decades.[14] In tracing the history of atheism, Alister McGrath calls it 'one of the greatest and most distressing paradoxes of human history' that in the twentieth century 'the greatest intolerance and violence of that century were practised by those who believed that religion caused intolerance and violence'.[15]

Why is Dawkins unwilling to face the truth about atheism's gruesome track record?

## On the other hand ...

He goes to great lengths in listing evils in which religion was an issue, yet barely mentions a single benefit that has flowed from religious faith and avoids giving appropriate credit to Christians who pioneered enormous social benefits. He mentions slavery, but not William Wilberforce, whose Christian convictions motivated him to have the slave trade abolished. He ignores Elizabeth Fry, who pioneered prison reform in Britain and Europe; the Seventh Earl of Shaftesbury, who laboured to improve working conditions during and after the Industrial Revolution; the evangelical Jean Henri Dunant, whose writing inspired the founding of the Red Cross; and Thomas Barnardo, who provided housing for 60,000 needy children and material help for another 250,000. He lists the civil rights activist Martin Luther King among political leaders, but ignores the Christian convictions which shaped his civil rights work and were reflected in his last major speech, when he summed up his passion with the words: 'I just want to do God's will.'

These headline names represent countless other Christian believers who today sacrifice their material possessions, and sometimes their lives, in the service of others, fight AIDS and other major diseases, campaign against poverty and injustice and do a tremendous amount of work to reduce Third World debt. Is there something significant about Dawkins ignoring all of this? Michael Shermer, President of the Skeptics Society, takes a much more honest approach and acknowledges that, for every one of the 'grand tragedies' in which religion has been implicated, 'there are ten thousand acts of personal good and social kindness that go unreported'.[16]

In trying to link Christianity and violence Dawkins turns the biblical text on its head. For example, he builds on the American physician John Hartung's idea that Jesus signed up to 'in-group morality' and 'out-group hostility', then claims that when Jesus taught his followers, 'Love your neighbour' (Matthew 19:19) he meant only, 'Love another Jew.'[17] This bizarre idea suggests that Jesus promoted racism by excluding all non-Jews, but it directly contradicts what Jesus taught. In answer to a Jewish lawyer's question, 'Who is my neighbour?' he told of a Jew attacked by robbers and left for dead on a country roadside. Two passing Jews did nothing to help, but the man was rescued by a Samaritan. This was remarkable, as there was bitter enmity between the Samaritans and the Jews, yet Jesus then told his questioner, 'You go, and do likewise' (Luke 10:37). The message is crystal clear: we are to be kind and compassionate to all those in need, regardless of our ethnic, religious or cultural differences. Assuming he read the parable, how could Dawkins possibly interpret it as meaning exactly the opposite?

Dawkins also claims that taking 'direct instruction, for example through the Ten Commandments,' would encourage a system of morals which any civilized modern person would find 'obnoxious'.[18] He quotes 'New Ten Commandments' from an atheist website and suggests a few of his own, the first of which encourages any form of sexual behaviour in private, 'so long as it damages nobody else'.[19] Yet do the original Ten Commandments (see Exodus 20:1–17) really produce an 'obnoxious' result? Given the full biblical meaning of even the last six, let us imagine a society that kept them. There would be no broken families, no harsh parenting, no teenage rebellion, no sidelining of grandparents, no murder, no violence, no hatred, no aggression, no unrighteous anger, no degradation of human life, no child abuse, no character assassination, no abortion on demand, no euthanasia, no suicide, no adultery, no children conceived outside of marriage, no sexual impurity in thought, word or action, no sodomy, no prostitution, no incest, no obscenity, no stealing, no dishonesty, no sharp practice in business dealings, no self-indulgence at the expense of others, no lying, no slander, no perjury, no rumour-mongering, no covetousness, no envy, no greed, no materialism. Would Dawkins have a problem with this kind of society?

# 5

# God:

# necessary or non-existent?

'The New Atheism', of which Dawkins is a leading representative, has recently gathered pace as an aggressive political and social movement. It insists that religion is the cause of most of the world's evil, that God has never existed and that to believe in him is wicked and dangerous ignorance. Specifically, it says that the Christian faith should be wiped out and that science can explain everything.

As one of its cheerleaders, Dawkins snipes at God throughout *The God Delusion*, but in chapter 2 he pulls out all the stops: 'The God of the Old Testament is arguably the most unpleasant character in all fiction: jealous and proud of it; a petty, unjust, unforgiving control freak; a vindictive, bloodthirsty ethnic cleanser; a misogynistic, homophobic, racist, infanticidal, genocidal, filicidal, pestilential, megalomaniacal, sadomasochistic, capriciously malevolent bully.'[1] In spite of his earlier promise, 'I shall not go out of my way to offend,'[2] this may be the most offensive and concentrated attack on God ever recorded in print. It is mounted with such passion that two words in his avalanche of adjectives are not even found in *The Oxford Dictionary of English* (though we can get the gist of what they mean), yet in the following paragraph Dawkins claims that he is 'not attacking [God's] particular qualities'![3] In fact, he fails to land a single blow on the God revealed in the Bible, but merely attacks his own distorted caricature of God. As Francis Collins puts it, 'Dawkins is a master of setting up a straw man, and then dismantling it with great relish.'[4]

An open-minded study of the Bible soon defuses Dawkins' attack. For example, he calls God 'an unforgiving control freak'. To call God 'unforgiving' is curious to say the least, as the Bible teems with evidence to the contrary. It records a national day of remembrance and celebration on which Israel's leaders showed the nation's history to be crammed with evidence that God is 'ready to forgive, gracious and merciful, slow to anger and abounding in steadfast love' (Nehemiah 9:17). To describe God as a 'control freak' is a contradiction in terms. The Bible certainly makes it clear that he 'works all things according to the counsel of his will' (Ephesians 1:11), and that 'his kingdom rules over all' (Psalm 103:19), but if God is not *by definition* in sovereign control of all other realities, he is merely one of countless deities, each with its own 'parish'. Nothing could be further from the Bible's teaching.

Chapter 4 of *The God Delusion* gets to 'the central argument'[5] of the book. In a nutshell it runs like this: there seems to be amazing design in the natural world; evolution shows this to be an illusion; and arguing for a designer poses the problem of 'Who designed the designer?' Dawkins produces this as the 'killer question', but I have it heard time and again (often abbreviated to 'Who created God?') not only at hundreds of all-age meetings, but even at kindergarten level.

The answer to it begins with yet another question: Which god do you mean? If you mean one of the ancient Greek or Roman deities such as Aphrodite, Eros, Jupiter or Neptune the answer is easy, as each one is man-made and, in the Bible's words, 'has no real existence' (1 Corinthians 8:4). Like all other gods littering religious history, their names represent nothing more than ideas invented by men. The difference between them and the one true God could not be greater: 'For all the gods of the peoples are worthless idols, but the Lord made the heavens' (Psalm 96:5). An Old Testament prophet rightly mocked the folly of those who put any trust in the man-made deities of his time:

Their idols are like scarecrows in a cucumber field,
    and they cannot speak;
they have to be carried
    for they cannot walk …
[They] are false,
    and there is no breath in them.
They are worthless, *a work of delusion*
(Jeremiah 10:5,14–15, emphasis added).

This means that while one could talk in terms of 'The Aphrodite Delusion' or 'The Jupiter Delusion', to speak of 'The God Delusion' is another matter. Asking, 'Who created God?' is in the same league as asking, 'If God is all-powerful, could he make a stone so heavy that he would not be able to lift it?' I have also heard this used as a 'killer question', but it makes no sense, because if there is an irresistible force there cannot be an immovable object, and if there is an immovable object there cannot be an irresistible force. The 'killer question' is nonsensical, as it really asks, 'Who created the uncreated God?'

The root of the problem here is Dawkins' assumption that if God exists he must have been created, but this wrecks his entire argument. As atheist philosopher Thomas Nagel shows, Dawkins' arguments would be worth considering only if God were 'a supremely adept and intelligent natural being, with a super-body and a super-brain'.[6] Suggesting that 'The existence of God is a scientific hypothesis like any other'[7] makes matters worse, as it ignores the Bible's teaching that God is *by definition* not part of the natural world, but is infinite, uncreated, beyond all restrictions of time and space and beyond science's reach. He is 'the eternal God' (Deuteronomy 33:27) and is 'from everlasting to everlasting' (Psalm 106:48), the only truly independent reality and the source of all creation. What is more, 'God is spirit' (John 4:24), with no material or physical properties or features. Although I do not share all his views on evolution, Francis Collins makes a powerful point here: 'If God exists, then he must be outside the natural world, and therefore the tools of science are not the right ones to learn about him.'[8] The renowned science writer Stephen J. Gould confirmed 'for the umpteenth millionth time' that as far as the existence of God was concerned, 'we simply can't comment on it as scientists'.[9] Many eminent scientists could be quoted along the same lines, yet Dawkins claims to settle the issue by virtually denying God's existence. This shortens the discussion but leaves all the questions unanswered, including this one: why should God require *any* explanation?

When Dawkins claims (without a shred of evidence) that he can show that God almost certainly does not exist because there can never be anything uncreated, he is arguing in circles. Everything that had a beginning had a cause, *but by definition God had no beginning.* The Bible's opening words are, 'In the beginning God ...' (Genesis 1:1). When sceptics respond by saying, 'But I can't understand the idea of infinity', I always reply, 'Join the club!' Infinity is not something our finite minds can grasp, but claiming that this rules out an eternal God is arrogance masquerading as intelligence. The argument is on the same level as that quoted in a 2009 letter to the *Daily Telegraph*, in which a mother reported her little girl as asking, 'Mummy, when God made the world, where did he stand?' We can forgive this from a six year-old, but a mature adult ought to do better.

Dawkins is angry and frustrated that so many persist in believing in God, but without a soundly based definition of God his entire argument falls flat on its face. His 'God' (a material being with a beginning in time) is certainly a delusion and can be tossed aside along with Eros, Jupiter and every other man-made deity. The God revealed in the Bible is totally different as he alone is the ultimate explanation for all other reality. C. S. Lewis said that he believed in God 'as I believe the sun has risen, not only because I see it, but because by it I see everything else'.[10]

## Odds against?

Elsewhere, Dawkins agrees with a blogger's definition of God as an 'unreachable, unknowable sky-fairy',[11] but at the 1992 Edinburgh International Science Festival he covered his back by saying, 'We cannot prove that there is no God, but we can safely conclude that he is very, very improbable indeed.' Yet even this interesting idea does not prove anything. The odds against each player having a complete suit at bridge is 2,235,197,406,895,366,368,301,559,999 to one—but it could happen! Then what does 'very, very improbable' mean? How can we decide levels of improbability? The distinguished British scientist Professor Edgar Andrews says that although Dawkins produces the improbability idea 'with a flourish' it 'holds no more water than a sieve'.[12] There is a vast difference between improbability and impossibility.

Scientifically speaking, a highly complex universe, yet one governed by the laws of nature, is extremely improbable—but it exists, governed as we have seen by ('very, very improbable'?) laws. Where did they come from? Can we settle for there being no explanation? Professor Keith Ward, a Fellow of the British Academy, shows where this kind of thinking leads: 'One day there might be nothing. The next day, there might be a very large carrot. Nothing else in existence whatsoever, all alone and larger than life, a huge carrot. If anything is possible, that certainly is. The day after that, the carrot might disappear and be replaced by a purple spotted gorilla. Why not? … Why does this thought seem odd, or even ridiculous, whereas the thought that some law of physics might just pop into existence does not? Logically, they are exactly on a par.'[13]

Stephen J. Gould called the arrival of mankind on our planet 'a wildly improbable evolutionary event'[14]—yet here we are! Does Dawkins rate God's existence more or less improbable than ours? How does he decide? Is it by logic or mathematics? As probability can never rule something in, so improbability can never rule something out, which means that however improbable Dawkins considers God to be, improbability is not a sound basis for atheism. In any case, God could exist without being required to prove or explain his existence. Keith Ward narrows the options: 'God is either necessary, and so God exists, or God is impossible, and so could not possibly exist.'[15] Denying God's existence on the basis of probability is no wiser than an announcement made by Moscow Radio on Christmas Day 1960: 'Our rocket has bypassed the moon and is nearing the sun, and we have not discovered God. We have turned out lights in heaven that no man will be able to put on again.'

Francis Collins was once (in his own words) 'an obnoxious atheist', but after reading C. S. Lewis's *Mere Christianity* he came to realize that his own arguments against faith in God 'were those of a schoolboy'.[16] As a world-class scientist, and long after becoming a Christian, he set out a solid basis for doing so: 'There are good reasons to believe in God, including the existence of mathematical principles and order in creation. They are positive reasons, based on knowledge.'[17]

'Who designed the designer?' is not a 'killer question'. It is the wrong question.

# 6

# The Bible:
# the book that speaks for
# itself

Dawkins says some very complimentary things about the Bible. He notes that the Authorized Version, first published in 1611, 'includes passages of outstanding literary merit in its own right' and commends it as 'a major source book for literary culture'.[1] Along the same lines he says, 'Surely ignorance of the Bible is bound to impoverish one's appreciation of literature?'[2] Yet these statements say nothing about the Bible's message or integrity, and when he addresses these he adopts a very different approach.

He is scathing about the Old Testament in general, though, as we saw earlier, he majors on a racy revamping of a few incidents which, when wrenched out of context, show God and his people in a very poor light. It is interesting to notice that in dealing with the Old Testament he avoids any mention of something that provides powerful evidence of its integrity. The Dead Sea Scrolls, 100 of them representing thirty-eight of the thirty-nine Old Testament books, were discovered between 1947 and 1956. Some of the scrolls date from 1,000 years earlier than the oldest text we had before 1947, yet the handwritten text, copied countless times over a period of ten centuries, remained virtually identical. For example, the difference in Isaiah 53, a particularly important Old Testament chapter, is just one word of three letters, and the change makes no difference to the meaning of the passage concerned. The accuracy of the Dead Sea Scrolls convinced F. F. Bruce, Rylands Professor of Biblical Criticism and Exegesis at the University of Manchester, that 'the Jewish scribes of the early Christian centuries copied and recopied the text of the Hebrew Bible with the utmost fidelity'.[3]

Turning to the New Testament, Dawkins assures us that the books we now have are nothing like the originals, which were 'copied and recopied' by 'fallible scribes' over generations of 'Chinese Whispers'.[4] This is a game in which information passed (often whispered) from one person to another can become badly distorted by the time it reaches the last player. In real life the same is often true about rumour or gossip, which can eventually bear little or no resemblance to the original story. Convinced that this is how the New Testament came to us, Dawkins dismisses it in one sentence: 'The only difference between *The Da Vinci Code* and the gospels is that the gospels are ancient fiction while *The Da Vinci Code* is modern fiction.'[5]

His fellow atheists may enjoy the clever sound bite, but there is no evidence that this is what happened. Dawkins' verdict seems to be driven by prejudice rather than principle, and experts in the field have easily demolished it. Sir William Ramsay was Professor of Classical Art and Architecture at Oxford University, Regius Professor of Humanity at Aberdeen University and a founder member of the British Academy. His early training led him to believe that the New Testament was a collection of myths, but after extensive field work in the Middle East, concentrating especially on Luke's contributions to the New Testament (the Gospel of Luke and the Acts of the Apostles), he concluded, 'Luke is a historian of the first rank' and 'should be placed along with the very greatest of historians.'[6] So a distinguished expert on the subject ranks Luke as a superb historian whose writings we can trust implicitly, while a critic with neither training nor expertise in the subject says Luke was playing Chinese Whispers. Who should we believe?

Like Dawkins, Simon Greenleaf, Royal Professor of Law at Harvard University, set out to destroy the credibility of the New Testament, but eventually determined that it is utterly reliable and that 'the attributes of truth are strikingly apparent throughout the Gospel histories'.[7] Donald Wiseman, Emeritus Professor of Assyriology at the University of London, asserted, 'No fact of archaeology so far discovered contradicts the biblical record.'[8] Sir Frederic Kenyon, one-time Director and Principal Librarian of the British Museum, came to this conclusion: 'The last foundation for any doubt that the Scriptures have come down to us as they were written has been removed. Both the authenticity and general integrity of the New Testament may be regarded as finally established.'[9]

## Falsehoods and facts

On one page of *The God Delusion* alone, when commenting on the birth of Jesus, Dawkins makes three statements that flatly contradict the Bible's record. Firstly, he says, 'When the gospels were written, many years after Jesus' death, nobody knew where he was born.'[10] One of the two Gospels recording the event says, 'Jesus was born in Bethlehem of Judea' (Matthew 2:1) and the other describes the birth as being in 'the city of David, which is called Bethlehem' (Luke 2:4), and as there is not a shred of evidence that this information was invented we have no reason for believing what Dawkins says.

Secondly, he quotes John as specifically pointing out that 'His followers were surprised that he was not born in Bethlehem.'[11] The passage he may have in mind records a discussion as to whether Jesus was the promised Messiah. Some thought he was, while others (assuming he had been born in the Galilean town of Nazareth, where he lived) said, 'Is the Christ to come from Galilee? Has not the Scripture said that the Christ comes ... from Bethlehem?' (John 7:41–42). At this point Jesus was not speaking to an inner circle of his own followers who already believed he was the Messiah, but to questioning crowds who were milling around in Jerusalem at that time. The Gospel writer merely records what people said, without commenting on their mistake. Dawkins fails to realize this, and so misses the whole point of the passage.

Thirdly, while Dawkins correctly reflects Matthew's record of the family's move to Nazareth after the birth of Jesus, he assumes without evidence that Mary and Joseph had been living in Bethlehem 'all along'.[12] Matthew says no such thing and we are told elsewhere that Mary and Joseph lived in Nazareth before Jesus was born (see Luke 1:26–27; 2:4) and merely went to Bethlehem because they were required to do so by the census.

Elsewhere, Dawkins claims that nobody knew who the writers of the four Gospels were and that 'they almost certainly never met Jesus personally'.[13] This would have surprised two of them (Matthew and John) as they were among Jesus' inner circle of disciples (see Matthew 4:21; 9:9) and hardly left his side for three years!

It gets worse. At one point Dawkins agrees with John Hartung's claim that 'It was Paul who invented the idea of taking the Jewish God to the Gentiles.'[14] Hardly! Long before Paul abandoned his terrorist campaign against the early church and became a Christian, let alone an apostle, Jesus told his followers to be his witnesses 'in Jerusalem and in all Judea and Samaria, and to the end of the earth' (Acts 1:8) and to 'make disciples of all nations' (Matthew 28:19)—and in any case it was Peter, not Paul, who first deliberately took the gospel to the Gentiles. How did Dawkins miss this? As Hartung cannot be trusted to tell us what the Bible says, he is hardly qualified to tell us what it means.

Dawkins also tells us that Luke records the baby Jesus being worshipped 'by kings'.[15] He is obviously referring to the 'wise men from the east' (Matthew 2:1) who went to Bethlehem and worshipped the child, but the Bible nowhere calls them kings (whatever the Christmas carol says). This part of *The God Delusion* is littered with so many mistakes that it is impossible to take the author seriously on the subject of the Bible's origin, text or meaning.

Writing about the Bible as a whole, Dawkins says it is 'just plain weird, as you would expect of a chaotically cobbled-together anthology of disjointed documents, composed, revised, translated, distorted and "improved" by hundreds of anonymous authors, editors and copyists'.[16] He offers no evidence for this, giving the impression that he has no historical understanding of how the Bible came into being. At one point he says, 'We pick and choose which bits of scripture to believe, which bits to write off as symbols or allegories,'[17] but those who read the Bible properly do no such thing. The Bible contains history, law (civil, criminal, ethical, ritual and sanitary), lyric, poetry, parable, symbol, allegory, biography, prophecy and several other forms of writing. To insist that the only way to read the Bible is to take every word literally and to treat its context as irrelevant is to sweep all of this aside. When such things as symbols or allegories are recognized as such they can properly be accepted on their own terms, then given the same authority as passages that are clearly meant to be taken literally. When we read that 'the windows of the heavens were opened' (Genesis 7:11) it would be as ridiculous to reject the statement because there are no windows in the sky as it would be to accuse God of cruelty to animals if a friend told us that in his part of the country it was 'raining cats and dogs'. Dawkins sweeps all of this aside and seems to ransack the Bible looking for bits that could be interpreted to support his agenda, regardless of context or style. This may explain why the influential literary critic Terry Eagleton writes that Dawkins and others like him 'invariably come up with vulgar caricatures of religious faith that would make a first-year theology student wince'.[18]

## Hallmarks

In *The God Delusion* Dawkins rounds off one section on the Bible by saying that 'we can give up belief in God while not losing touch with a treasured heritage,'[19] but this spectacularly ignores the Bible's insistence that God is not only its subject but *its author*. Phrases such as 'God said', 'God spoke' and 'The word of the Lord came' occur over 4,000 times in the Old Testament alone, including 700 times in the first five books and forty times in one chapter. Old Testament prophets had no hesitation in claiming that their message was to be treated as coming from God and not merely from his representatives. The apostle Paul, who wrote about half of the New Testament, endorsed their claim and called the Old Testament 'the very words of God' (Romans 3:2, NIV).

What is more, he claimed the same divine authority for his own ministry, assuring his readers that any spiritually mature person would recognize 'that the things I am writing to you are a command of the Lord' (1 Corinthians 14:37). Other New Testament heavyweights made similar claims. The apostle Peter said that the message he and his fellow prophets brought was 'sent from heaven' (1 Peter 1:12), while the apostle John plainly stated that what he wrote was 'the word of God' (Revelation 1:2).

Sceptics could argue that mentally deranged people have sometimes been known to make bizarre claims about their identity and 'message', but none of the men who committed the Bible's message to writing fits this sad bill. The Bible's sixty-six books were written by some forty authors over a period of more than 1,500 years. They included kings, legislators, statesmen, priests, prophets and a physician, and their sanity has never been undermined. No other 'holy book' can match the Bible's prophetic accuracy, historical integrity or amazing unity. The Bible not only claims to be the Word of God, it gives us good reasons for believing that its claim is true and can therefore be trusted. The contemporary American philosopher and theologian John Frame rightly maintains, 'If God's speech has an obvious location that location must be in the Holy Scriptures. There simply is no other candidate.'[20]

To call the Bible 'a chaotically cobbled-together anthology of disjointed documents' is rather like judging a piece of classical music after hearing the orchestra tune up. The distinguished British theologian J. I. Packer is a much safer guide to the Bible's unity and harmony. With over half a century of study to draw on, he writes:

The Bible appears like a symphony orchestra, with the Holy Spirit as its Toscanini; each instrumentalist has been brought willingly, spontaneously, creatively to play his notes just as the great conductor desired, in full harmony with each other, though none of them could ever hear the music as a whole.[21]

This makes a powerful point. A mixture of truth and fiction never holds together in this way, but consistent truth always does and Dawkins is clearly blind to the unifying themes that bind the Bible's different parts together and reveal God's unfolding purposes for mankind—and to the fundamental truth that, far from being a collection of men's ideas, 'All Scripture is breathed out by God' (2 Timothy 3:16).

# 7

# Christianity:
# evidence and effects

The God Delusion is a broadside against all religion, but Dawkins says Christianity is its main target because 'it is the version with which I happen to be most familiar'.[1] However, 'most familiar' has a hollow ring to it when this opening definition makes three fundamental errors in one sentence: 'Christianity was founded by Paul of Tarsus as a less ruthlessly monotheistic sect of Judaism.'[2]

Firstly, to call Paul the founder of Christianity is laughable, when the Bible tells us that before his conversion he was 'ravaging the church, and entering house after house, he dragged off men and women and committed them to prison' (Acts 8:3). After being arrested for his work as an apostle, he testified that in his unconverted days he was 'opposing the name of Jesus of Nazareth' and punishing Christians 'in raging fury against them' (Acts 26:9, 11). He even supported the execution of Stephen, Christianity's first martyr (see Acts 8:1). To call Paul the founder of Christianity is to turn history on its head. Paul himself says of the Christian church, 'No one can lay a foundation other than that which is laid, which is Jesus Christ' (1 Corinthians 3:11).

Secondly, calling Christianity 'less ruthlessly monotheistic' than Judaism is equally wrong. Monotheism, the belief that only one God exists, was the bedrock of Judaism throughout the Old Testament. 'Hear, O Israel: The LORD our God, the LORD is one' (Deuteronomy 6:4) is the first sentence of the famous *Shema*, which is at the heart of Jewish life, and Christianity never veered from this. Jesus firmly endorsed the *Shema* (see Mark 12:29), as did Paul when stating, 'There is no God but one' (1 Corinthians 8:4). Christianity is clearly monotheistic, though its essential distinctive is the Bible's teaching that, while God is one Being, he exists in three persons—the Father, the Son (Jesus) and the Holy Spirit. This Godhead (often called the Holy Trinity) is not a committee, with the Father in the chair, but three divine persons of equal glory and power.

Thirdly, to describe Christianity as a 'sect of Judaism' is to rewrite history. The Christian faith was certainly rooted in the Old Testament and held to a number of

Judaism's core beliefs, including one God as the creator and sustainer of the universe, mankind's accountability to him and the divine inspiration of the Old Testament. In its earliest days it even shared places of worship with Judaism, but it soon became clear that Christianity held to several key doctrines rejected by Judaism. These include the divine inspiration of the New Testament, the Holy Trinity, the identity of Jesus as Messiah and his virgin birth and resurrection; these alone make it impossible to consider Christianity as a sect of Judaism.

Dawkins follows these errors by telling us that, as an 'eccentric cult', Christianity 'was spread by the sword',[3] not only during the first century but for centuries afterwards by 'European invaders and colonists, with missionary accompaniment'.[4] Once again, Dawkins is wide of the mark. For the first three centuries of the Christian church, Christians were a persecuted minority and never in a position to spread their faith by the sword. Nobody can deny that in later centuries religious and political leaders sometimes used violence to promote their version of Christianity, but this never reflected Jesus' teaching or example, nor that of the New Testament as a whole.

While Jesus was rightly angry when driving unscrupulous traders and swindlers from the temple at Jerusalem (see Matthew 21:12–17; John 2:13–22), there is no record that he assaulted anyone, not even his bitterest enemies. He experienced violence, but was never violent.

When he was slandered, arrested, mocked, flogged, tortured and crucified he never once retaliated. When one of his followers cut off an enemy's ear Jesus told him, 'No more of this!', then miraculously restored the victim's ear (see Luke 22:51). None of the instructions he gave to the first Christians suggested coercion of any kind. Professing Christians have sometimes imposed their beliefs violently, but this has always been contrary to Jesus' instructions to his followers: 'Love your enemies, do good to those who hate you, bless those who curse you, pray for those who abuse you' (Luke 6:27–28). Linking genuine Christianity with man-made corruptions of it is being dishonest.

## Another bad miss

By including Christianity in a target for one particular assault, Dawkins makes another serious mistake. Writing in *The Guardian* a month after the 9/11 terrorist attacks in the United States, he claimed, 'Revealed faith is not harmless nonsense, it can be lethally dangerous. Dangerous because it gives people unshakeable confidence in their own righteousness.'[5] His fellow atheist Christopher Hitchens says much the same thing: 'Religion teaches people to be extremely self-centred and conceited.'[6] I cannot speak for other faiths, but Christianity does exactly the opposite. Jesus began his famous Sermon on the Mount with the words: 'Blessed are the poor in spirit, for theirs is the kingdom of heaven' (Matthew 5:3). To be 'poor in spirit' is to have a deep sense of one's own moral and spiritual bankruptcy, something Jesus said was the hallmark of a genuine Christian. He repeatedly condemned pride and taught, 'Whoever exalts himself will be humbled, and whoever humbles himself will be exalted' (Matthew 23:12).

The history of the Christian church is full of striking illustrations of this. It was said of the Protestant martyr John Bradford, who in 1555 was burned at the stake in Smithfield, London, that scarcely a day passed in which he did not weep over his sin. David Brainerd, the outstanding eighteenth-century missionary to the American Indians, said when at the peak of his ministry, 'There seemed to be nothing but sin and corruption within me.' George Whitefield (1714–1770) has been called the greatest preacher England ever produced, yet pleaded, 'Let my name be forgotten, let me be trodden under the feet of all men.' John Newton (1725–1807), the slave trader turned Anglican clergyman (now best known by many as the author of the hymn 'Amazing Grace'), wrote, 'Though I know in theory what a Christian should be, I am sadly deficient in practice! I see much to be ashamed of every day and in every circumstance.' Some 'revealed faith' religions may encourage self-righteousness; biblical Christianity does the opposite. Even the finest believers can lapse into pride from time to time, but the Bible directs them to 'do justice, and to love kindness, and to walk humbly with your God' (Micah

6:8). A persistently arrogant Christian is a contradiction in terms.

In the Old Testament, King David explains why this is the case: 'Behold, I was brought forth in iniquity; and in sin did my mother conceive me' (Psalm 51:5). David is saying that he is no different from any other human being—a sinner from the moment of conception. This infuriates those who reject the doctrine of original sin, but is clearly confirmed by the fact that no parent has to teach a child how to act wrongly. Even those who train young people to be terrorists are only channelling their sinful bias in a certain direction.

There was a time when Paul had been convinced that his religious upbringing and 'goodness' commended him to God, but becoming a Christian transformed his thinking. Far from boasting in his own righteousness, he now counted all his religious achievements as 'rubbish' and trusted not in 'a righteousness of my own' but in one 'which comes through faith in Christ' (Philippians 3:8–9). Elsewhere he confessed, 'I know that nothing good lives in me, that is, in my sinful nature' (Romans 7:18, NIV).

These testimonies disprove Dawkins' claim. All other world faiths have what amounts to a 'points system' for achieving whatever goal they present; Christianity does the opposite. Uniquely, it sets the bar impossibly high by saying that 'The law of the Lord is perfect' (Psalm 19:7), then confirms that we have all come short because 'Whoever keeps the whole law but fails in one point has become accountable for all of it' (James 2:10). Christianity makes it clear that God's law is not a set of rules challenging us to get a pass mark and condemning us if we fail. Instead, it is given to make us conscious that by nature, desire and action we have broken it repeatedly (see Romans 3:19–20) and constantly 'fall short of the glory of God' (Romans 3:23).

This hardly corresponds with Dawkins' accusation about self-righteousness, but it raises an important question: 'How can the Christian message be called "the gospel" (good news) when it begins by condemning the entire human race?' The answer lies in a phrase which *The God Delusion* never addresses and of which I assume Dawkins has no understanding—'the grace of God'. This is so amazing that the Bible calls its riches 'immeasurable' (Ephesians 2:7), but this will point us in the right direction: *the grace of God is his unmerited favour to sinners.* The Bible says, 'The grace of God has appeared, bringing salvation for all people' (Titus 2:11). It is offered to all without exception and those who receive it are transformed. They become convinced that they are guilty of breaking God's law; their denials, scepticism and doubts are replaced with faith in Jesus Christ; they have a longing to turn from sin and increasingly do so; and they become assured of God's forgiveness and of their acceptance into his eternal family. This is what Paul meant when he told first-century Christians, 'For by grace you have been saved through faith. And this is not your own doing; it is the gift of God, not a result of works, so that no one may boast' (Ephesians 2:8–9). Is there any sign of self-righteousness there? The Christian church is not a showroom for superstars, but a fellowship of recovering sinners at various stages of spiritual progress.

Another high-profile atheist, Sam Harris, dismisses theology as 'little more than a branch of human ignorance,'[7] and Dawkins agrees: 'The entire thrust of my position is that Christian theology is a non-subject. It is empty. Vacuous. Devoid of coherence or content.'[8] This is hardly surprising, but, as his fellow atheist Thomas Nagel confirms, when commenting on theology, 'Dawkins is operating mostly outside the range of his scientific expertise.'[9] In reviewing *The God Delusion*, Terry Eagleton concluded that reading Dawkins on theology was like hearing 'someone holding forth on biology whose only knowledge of the subject is the *Book of British Birds*'.[10]

Genuine Christianity is grounded in history and endorsed by its evidence and effects. All of Dawkins' attacks leave it unscathed.

# Jesus:
# the man for all reasons

Christianity is the only world faith based on the identity of its founder, rather than on his teachings, which means that anybody wanting to destroy Christianity must deal with Jesus Christ. Dawkins gives himself room to manoeuvre by suggesting that Jesus 'probably existed,'[1] but this ignores more than a hundred facts about Jesus recorded by nearly twenty celebrated first-century commentators, many of them pagans. History does not appear to be Dawkins' strong suit. He tells us that United States President Thomas Jefferson, who died in 1826, encouraged his nephew to read a number of 'Gospels'[2] that only came to light in 1945, having been lost for nearly 2,000 years, and in any case these so-called 'Gnostic Gospels' were never accepted by the Christian church as having divine authority. Clearer minds have concluded that the evidence for Jesus is overwhelming; the scientific genius Albert Einstein rightly said, 'No man can deny that Jesus existed.'[3]

While claiming to focus mainly on Christianity in writing *The God Delusion*, everything he says about its founder takes up less than five pages and much of what he says is pure invention. Firstly, he writes, 'There is no good historical evidence that [Jesus] ever thought he was divine,'[4] yet this flatly contradicts the evidence. I have reviewed this elsewhere[5] and there is room here for just one example, which is unusually strong because it comes from contemporary Jewish enemies of Jesus. When they wanted to stone him to death, and Jesus asked them (tongue in cheek?) which of his 'many good works' had led them to this, they replied, 'It is not for a good work that we are going to stone you but for blasphemy, because you, being a man *make yourself God*' (John 10:32–33, emphasis added). Why does Dawkins ignore this?

Secondly, Dawkins says that Jesus 'explicitly departed' from Old Testament writings,[6] but this is an amazing twisting of the truth. In discussing the Old Testament Jesus often used the phrase, 'You have heard that it was said …' before adding, 'But I say to you …' (e.g. Matthew 5:21–22, 27–28, 43–44). At first sight this seems to prove Dawkins' point, though this is not the case. Jesus was correcting not the Old Testament but the legalistic 'spin' that religious scholars had put on it. 'But I say to you …' always introduced the true meaning of the text, based on the principles that lay behind it. Far from contradicting the Old Testament, Jesus frequently clinched an issue by pinning his hearers to what it said and meant (e.g. Matthew 4:4; Mark 14:27; Luke 19:46).

He also endorsed Old Testament writings by stating, 'I have not come to abolish them but to fulfil them' (Matthew 5:17). Did Dawkins miss this? After reading an Old Testament prophecy about the coming of God's Messiah, Jesus was referring to himself when he told synagogue worshippers in Nazareth, 'Today this Scripture has been fulfilled in your hearing' (Luke 4:21), while elsewhere he said that all the Old Testament writings 'bear witness about me' (John 5:39). How can this possibly mean that he 'departed' from what the Old Testament said?

Thirdly, there is the death of Jesus, which even Dawkins recognizes as involving 'the central doctrine of Christianity'.[7] He calls the idea that Jesus died to atone for the sins of others not only 'morally obnoxious'[8] and 'vicious, sado-masochistic and repellent'[9] but 'barking mad'.[10] He seems to interpret the Bible as teaching that Jesus was an innocent third party wrongly punished by God for the sins of others, but this is not the case. Jesus was not executed against his will; as he told his followers, 'No one takes [my life] from me, but I lay it down of my own accord' (John 10:18). Nor was God punishing Jesus for his sin; far from deserving God's anger, Jesus was able to claim, 'I always do the things that are pleasing to him' (John 8:29). The sins for which Jesus was punished were the sins of others; as Peter put it, 'He himself bore our sins in his body' (1 Peter 2:24).

What is more, God was not punishing a third party (which *would* be 'morally obnoxious') but, as Jesus was God in human form, God was taking the punishment upon himself. As the contemporary British author John Stott puts it, 'He laid aside his immunity to pain. He entered our world of flesh and blood, tears and death. He suffered for us.'[11] Nor was this amazing act of love a desperate attempt to retrieve a situation that had got out of hand. Instead, it was planned in heaven 'before the foundation of the world' (1 Peter 1:20). Far from being an unavoidable tragedy, Jesus was 'delivered up according to the definite plan and foreknowledge of God' (Acts 2:23). Yet Dawkins bizarrely suggests that Jesus allowed himself to be tortured and executed merely 'to impress himself'.[12]

One other thing: although crucifixion was a horrific form of execution, the worst suffering Jesus endured on the cross was not physical but spiritual. When the Bible speaks of 'the law of sin and death' (Romans 8:2), the death referred to is both physical and spiritual—and Jesus suffered both. His physical death was obvious, but his spiritual death, though 'invisible', was much worse. In Jesus' death 'God made him who had no sin to be sin for us' (2 Corinthians 5:21, NIV), and such was the appalling punishment he bore in his body and spirit that he cried out, 'My God, my God, why have you forsaken me?' (Matthew 27:46). No human being has ever endured greater suffering. In a way that is beyond our imagination he sensed that the perfect harmony he had enjoyed with his Father throughout eternity had been shattered.

Yet Jesus' crucifixion was not a disaster. As Isaiah had prophesied centuries earlier:

> He was wounded for our transgressions;
> > he was crushed for our iniquities;
> upon him was the chastisement that brought us peace,
> > and with his stripes we are healed
> (Isaiah 53:5).

In Paul's words, 'Christ redeemed us from the curse of the law by becoming a curse for us' (Galatians 3:13). Dawkins responds to this by asking, 'If God wanted to forgive our sins, why not just forgive them?',[13] but this is an absurd idea, as no reasonable justice system lets offenders off the hook in this way. How could God do so when 'Righteousness and justice are the foundation of his throne'? (Psalm 97:2).

## Man alive!

The meaning of the atoning death of Jesus is clarified by what happened three days later, an event about which

Dawkins says virtually nothing. When I asked an atheist student at the University of Cape Town, 'What do you think of Jesus Christ?' he immediately replied, 'I am not sure, but I do know this: everything hinges on whether or not he rose again from the dead.' He was right. If Jesus did not rise again his birth, life and death would leave us with nothing more than a buried collection of bones and dust. Yet having asked, 'Did [Jesus] come alive again, three days after being crucified?'[14] Dawkins ignores the subject! He refuses to examine the evidence, relying instead on his theory that it never happened. This hardly suggests a scientist committed to following the evidence wherever it leads.

This weird imbalance is a feature of *The God Delusion*. For instance, it refers repeatedly to homosexuality, which is a serious issue, but has nothing to do with the subject of the book. Elsewhere, an entire chapter of more than thirty pages rails against child abuse. No normal person would deny that this is a sickening crime, but again it does not relate to the subject of the book.

In a interview for the *Independent* Dawkins said, 'Accounts of Jesus' resurrection are about as well documented as Jack and the Beanstalk,'[15] while elsewhere he called the resurrection story 'petty, trivial and local' and 'parochial'.[16] Yet the Bible teaches that the resurrection eventually leads to the moment when Jesus will judge all humankind (see Acts 17:31) and when, willingly or unwillingly, all 'in heaven and on earth and under the earth' will acknowledge 'that Jesus Christ is Lord, to the glory of God the Father' (Philippians 2:10–11). Can this be called petty, trivial, local and parochial?

For Dawkins to call the question of the resurrection of Jesus 'strictly scientific'[17] is equally absurd; it is not scientific, but historical—and it has been said that there is more documentary evidence for the resurrection of Jesus than for the Roman invasion of Britain, recorded in just a few manuscripts, the earliest dating some 900 years after the event. I have examined the evidence for the resurrection of Jesus elsewhere;[18] only some of it can be given here.

Six independent witnesses record eleven different resurrection appearances. On one occasion over 500 saw Jesus alive after death, and when Paul wrote about this some time later over half of them were still alive and could have confirmed this (see 1 Corinthians 15:6). Sceptics have suggested that sightings of Jesus were hallucinations, but a medical expert confirms that 'The resurrection appearances break every known law of visions.'[19]

His closest followers, hiding away for fear of being next on the religious authorities' hit list, were suddenly prepared to face persecution, torture, imprisonment and execution rather than deny that they had met with the risen Jesus. That Jesus might rise from the dead was something they were previously unable to grasp, even when Jesus had prophesied that he would. If their testimonies had been concocted they would have rapidly changed their story when their own lives were at risk. Religious fanatics—suicide bombers, for instance—have been prepared to die for things they believe to be true, but nobody is ever prepared to die for something they know to be false. A modern academic has called the disciples' transformation 'by far and away the strongest circumstantial evidence for the resurrection.'[20]

Christian churches form the largest religious group the world has ever known, with a current membership of two billion. The key to the church's existence is not a particular take on the nature of God, a unique theory about how the world came into being, or new religious rituals, but the bodily resurrection of Jesus. This distinguishes Christians from every other religious grouping the world has ever known. As someone has said, 'The Christian church has resurrection written all over it.'[21]

In spite of shameful episodes in the church's history, no other movement has been such a powerful influence for good. Prison reform, the abolition of the slave trade, the transformation of working conditions, the foundation of schools, hospitals and centres for the care of the homeless, the destitute and those rejected by the rest of society are part of its record, all of it driven by the resurrection of Jesus. As the American preacher D. James Kennedy noted, 'The Grand Canyon wasn't caused by an Indian dragging a stick, and the Christian church wasn't created by a myth.'[22]

After visiting Malawi in 2008, *The Times* journalist Matthew Parris said that, although he was 'a confirmed atheist', he had become convinced that Christian missionaries met a deeper need than all the financial aid being poured into Africa.[23] Lord Darling, a former Chief Justice of England, concluded, 'In its favour as a living truth there exists such overwhelming evidence, positive and negative, factual and circumstantial, that no intelligent jury could fail to bring in a verdict that the resurrection story is true.'[24] As a modern writer says, ignoring the resurrection of Jesus, then claiming to have dismantled Christianity, is like chasing mice out of the sitting-room and announcing that the house is free of animals, 'while there is an elephant grinning on the sofa!'[25]

## Just a man?

In the 1973 musical *Jesus Christ Superstar* Mary Magdalene sings of Jesus, 'He's a man. He's just a man.' His virgin conception, perfect life, substitutionary death and unique resurrection tell a very different story, and the Bible's testimony to his divinity goes far beyond these, not least in ascribing to him attributes that are true only of God. In the Old Testament, God is said to be 'from everlasting to everlasting' (Psalm 90:2); in the New Testament, Jesus has the title 'the Alpha and the Omega, the first and the last, the beginning and the end' (Revelation 22:13). In the Old Testament, God is said to be 'majestic in holiness' (Exodus 15:11); in the New Testament, Jesus is called 'the Holy One of God' (John 6:69). In the Old Testament we read of God that his understanding is 'beyond measure' (Psalm 147:5); in the New Testament we are told that Jesus possesses 'all the treasures of wisdom and knowledge' (Colossians 2:3). In the Old Testament, God says, 'I the LORD do not change' (Malachi 3:6); in the New Testament we read that Jesus is 'the same yesterday and today and for ever' (Hebrews 13:8). These are just some of the many examples of Jesus having attributes that can only be true of God.

It is said that actions speak louder than words, and the Bible records things done by Jesus that go far beyond even his miracles of healing. Two examples speak for many others. The Bible's opening words are, 'In the beginning God created the heavens and the earth' (Genesis 1:1); Paul writes of Jesus, 'By him all things were created, in heaven and on earth, visible and invisible … all things were created through him and for him' (Colossians 1:16). Far from him being an absentee landlord, the Bible says, 'The LORD has established his throne in the heavens, and his kingdom rules over all' (Psalm 103:19); it also says that Jesus 'upholds the universe by the word of his power'

(Hebrews 1:3). These attributes and actions of Jesus are just some of the ways in which the Bible portrays Jesus, not merely as a man, but as being 'the true God and eternal life' (1 John 5:20).

# 9

# Faith: beyond the facts

In many of his writings Dawkins rightly expresses
the value of evidence-based thinking and contrasts
this approach with that of believers in God, describing
their faith as 'blind trust, in the absence of evidence, even
in the teeth of evidence'.[1] Elsewhere he says, 'I think a
case can be made that faith is one of the world's great
evils, comparable to the smallpox virus but harder to
eradicate,'[2] and labels faith 'a kind of mental illness'.[3]

In the course of his crusade against Christianity,
Dawkins puts belief in God on a par with believing
in Santa Claus, the Tooth Fairy, fairies at the bottom
of the garden (one of his favourite examples), the
Flying Spaghetti Monster, or a china teapot orbiting
the sun (another favourite, borrowed from the British
philosopher Bertrand Russell).[4] This is good knockabout
stuff, but contributes nothing to a subject on which
Dawkins is clearly out of his depth. Psychiatrist Kathleen

Jones says more accurately, 'When we talk about our own faith, we mean what we personally believe in as a result of using common sense, logic and experience. We do not mean superstition, wishful thinking, self-delusion.'[5]

Several points can be made in response to Dawkins. A recent survey suggests that of six billion people in the world today, over five billion believe in God. We know that the Flying Spaghetti Monster is a ridiculous parody of religion, and Santa Claus, the Tooth Fairy and the rest exist only in juvenile imagination. As a child I had a 'belief' in Santa Claus only because bulging parcels appeared at the bottom of my bed early on Christmas Day, but I gave up when I found he was married to my mother! I have never met anyone who continued to believe in these myths (or began to believe in them) as adults. While numbers can be tweaked to prove almost anything, the convictions of five billion believers can hardly be ranked with flying teapots and the like. If the evidence for God was the same as for the Tooth Fairy, how many mature adults would believe in him?

Dawkins' definition of faith is an eccentric invention on his part. Having studied Christianity for over fifty years, I have found no church's definition of faith that even hints at it. Nor in interacting with countless Christians all around the world have I come across even one who would recognize it. This is another case of Dawkins creating a straw man and then taking great delight in demolishing it. This may pass as a child's game, but the subject is much too serious to treat like this. Alister McGrath is not exaggerating when he says that Dawkins' views on the nature of faith 'are best regarded as an embarrassment to anyone concerned with scholarly accuracy'.[6] When we turn from fallacy to fact and look honestly at what the Bible says about Christian faith we will soon discover that it means far more than simply accepting certain things as being true. We will also see that it has life-changing and eternal effects and implications.

## Reality

Firstly, the Christian faith requires that we accept the existence of God, and here the Bible endorses plain common sense: 'Whoever would draw near to God must believe that he exists' (Hebrews 11:6). How could it be otherwise? As it is impossible to *prove* the existence of God in the same way that one might prove the truth of a scientific theory or a mathematical equation, we should ask where the evidence *points*—and there is evidence galore. The universe has no scientific reason for existing; time and space are part of reality; and universal, elegant and consistent laws of nature are amazingly and precisely suited to allow life on our planet. How can these be explained in natural terms? The Bible's explanation for them is reflected in words inscribed on the entrance to the Cavendish Laboratory at Cambridge University when it was opened in 1874: 'The works of the Lord are great.' In Stephen Hawking's opinion, 'It would be very difficult to explain why the universe should have begun in this way, except as the act of a God who intended to create beings like us.'[7] Keith Ward believes that 'God is the best final explanation there can be for the universe.'[8]

The evidence mounts. Each one of us is composed of 100 trillion living cells, each resembling a sophisticated molecular factory; we have a sense of moral values which neither science nor evolution can explain; we have minds that enable us to make sense of things. We also have a mysterious spiritual dimension. Even the entrenched atheist Bertrand Russell conceded, 'The centre of me is always and eternally ... searching for something beyond what the world contains.'[9] How can we explain these things? Unless we allow prejudice to throttle our thinking, they point us to an uncaused, eternal reality that brought them into being. As the God revealed in the Bible fits the bill exactly, believing in him can hardly be called superstition or flying in the teeth of the evidence.

The Bible says that the universe reveals God's 'invisible attributes, namely his eternal power and divine nature', and that those who refuse to recognize this are 'without excuse' (Romans 1:19–20). In St Paul's Cathedral, London, the tomb of its architect, Sir Christopher Wren, has the Latin inscription: 'Reader: if you seek his monument, look around you.' God points us to creation and says the same kind of thing. As the modern author Stuart Olyott puts it, 'Nobody can plead that he is ignorant of the existence of God. It can clearly be seen that there is an Unseen.'[10] What of those who deny this? The Bible says that 'by their unrighteousness' they 'suppress the truth' (Romans 1:18). Whatever they may say, people do not deny God for scientific or philosophical reasons; unbelief has a *spiritual* root. Atheists *deliberately* do 'not honour ... God or give thanks to him' and do 'not see fit to acknowledge God' (Romans 1:21, 28). Biblical faith begins by accepting that God *is*.

Secondly, Christian faith also means believing not merely that God exists, but that Jesus Christ 'has made him known' (John 1:18). It means believing that Jesus is 'the true God and eternal life' (1 John 5:20) who 'came into the world to save sinners' (1 Timothy 1:15) and who alone can bridge the chasm between a holy Creator and an unholy creature. It also means believing that in his death Jesus bore the indescribable punishment for human sin, and that, though without any sin of his own, he 'suffered once for sins, the righteous for the unrighteous, that he might bring us to God' (1 Peter 3:18).

Thirdly, Christian faith goes beyond conviction and involves commitment. It is not enough to believe what the Bible says about Jesus. He is not a proposition but a person, and he demands a response that goes far beyond believing certain facts about him. Christian faith means committing oneself completely to him, trusting him alone to grant the forgiveness of sins and eternal life he promises.

Fourthly, Christian faith means rejecting any possibility of getting right with God on the basis of knowledge, moral achievements or anything else. As I know from my own experience, this can be very difficult, as it strikes at one's inbuilt pride. Sensing the need to get right with God, many trust in their religious background, their formal membership of a church, their knowledge of the Bible, their prayers, their giving to needy causes, or what they judge to be an acceptable moral standard of life. Yet the Bible says that, as far as getting right with God is concerned, 'All our righteous acts are like filthy rags' (Isaiah 64:6, NIV). No amount of good can remove the bad; in genuine Christian faith a person trusts solely in Jesus Christ.

Abandoning trust in one's own merits is part of what the Bible calls repentance, something tied so closely to faith that there can never be one without the other. Genuine faith always implies repentance, and genuine repentance always implies faith; the apostle Paul summed up his entire message by calling people to 'repentance towards God and ... faith in our Lord Jesus Christ' (Acts 20:21). To repent means much more than to confess one's sin. It involves shame, sorrow, regret, a distaste of sin for what it is (not just for the problems it causes) and a longing to lead a life that is God-centred instead of self-centred. The Bible gives a powerful incentive for true repentance:

> Let the wicked forsake his way,
>> and the unrighteous man his thoughts;
> let him return to the LORD,
> that he may have compassion on him,
>> and to our God, for he will abundantly pardon
> (Isaiah 55:7).

To be made right with God is not merely to know the forgiveness of sins here and now, but to be assured that after death one will escape God's deserved and everlasting punishment for sin and instead spend eternity in his glorious presence in heaven, where 'death shall be no more, neither shall there be mourning nor crying nor pain any more, for the former things have passed away' (Revelation 21:4).

This promise holds good for all who truly turn from sin and trust in Christ. It is offered to everyone without exception—including the religious hypocrite, the self-centred prig and the arrogant achiever, as well as the gentle do-gooder, the well-behaved citizen and the rebellious teenager. It is made to the agnostic, the sceptic and the atheist. There is no limit to the grace of God offered in the Christian gospel. Before he became a Christian the apostle Paul was 'a blasphemer, persecutor and insolent opponent' (1 Timothy 1:13); the great theologian Augustine was an immoral pagan; John Newton 'loved sin, and was unwilling to forsake it';[11] as we saw earlier, the world-famous scientist Francis Collins was once 'an obnoxious atheist'; and countless Christians (including the writer of this book) were dyed-in-the-wool religious hypocrites whose Christianity was a Sunday performance, not a daily experience.

God says. 'You will seek me and find me when you seek me with all your heart' (Jeremiah 29:13, NIV). The condition is clear and so is the promise. Everyone who is genuinely determined to find God and to commit their life to him will find him to be true to his word—even those who thought he was a delusion.

# Notes

## 1. The man and the mission

1.  Richard Dawkins, *The God Delusion*, Bantam Press, 2006, p. 261.

2.  Debate at the University of Alabama at Birmingham, 3 October 2007.

3.  Richard Dawkins, *The Selfish Gene*, Oxford University Press, p. 2.

4.  Dawkins, *The God Delusion*, p. 116.

5.  Ibid. p. 5.

6.  Ibid. p. 36.

7.  *Science and the Sacred*, 14 August 2009.

8.  These include Alister McGrath, *Dawkins' God* (Blackwell Publishing); Alister McGrath with Joanna Collicutt McGrath, *The Dawkins Delusion* (Society for Promoting Christian Knowledge); Scott Hahn and Benjamin Wiker, *Answering the New Atheism: Dismantling Dawkins' case against God* (Emmaus House Publishing); Kathleen Jones, *Challenging Richard Dawkins* (Canterbury Press); Edgar Andrews, *Who Made God?* (EP Books); David Robertson, *The Dawkins Letters* (Christian Focus Publications); Andrew Wilson, *Deluded by Dawkins?* (Kingsway Publications); Roger Steer, *Letters to an*

*Influential Atheist* (Authentic Lifestyle); Rob Slane, *The God Reality* (Day One Publications); Keith Ward, *Why There Almost Certainly is a God* (Lion Hudson); and Dinesh D'Souza, *What's so great about Christianity?* (Regnery Publishing).

## 2. Science: the answer to everything?

1.  Cited by N. McCullough, *Barriers to Belief*, Darton, Longman & Todd, p. 82.

2.  *Daily Telegraph Science Extra*, 11 September 1999.

3.  J. P. Moreland, *Scaling the Secular City*, Baker Book House, p. 3.

4.  See Richard P. Feynman, *What do you care what other people think?*, Unwin Hyman; and *The Meaning of it all*, Penguin Books.

5.  *Daily Telegraph*, 20 August 2009.

6.  BBC Radio Five Live, 22 September 2009.

7.  *Soul of Britain*, BBC Television, 11 June 2000.

8.  Cited by D. R. Alexander, 'Science: Friend or Foe?', *Cambridge Papers 4,3* (1995), p. 2.

9.  Alabama debate.

10. *New York Times*, 9 April 1989.

11. Dawkins, *The God Delusion*, p. 141.

12. Richard Dawkins, *The Blind Watchmaker*, Norton & Company, p. 139.

13. Dawkins, *The Selfish Gene*, p. 19.

14. Werner Gitt, *In the Beginning was Information*, Christliche Literatur, p. 79.

15. *Newsnight Review*, BBC 1, 9 September 2009.

16. Cited by Werner Gitt, *Did God use Evolution?*, Master Books, p. 24.

17. Stephen Hawking, *Black Holes and Baby Universes*, Bantam Books, p. 90.

18. Timothy Keller, *The Reason for God*, Hodder & Stoughton, p. 141.

19. Cited by Malcom W.Browne, *New York Times*, 12 March 1978.

20. Feynman, *What do you care what other people think?*

21. *Observer*, 9 April 1995.

22. Dawkins, *The Selfish Gene*, p. xxi.

23. Dawkins, *The Blind Watchmaker*, p. 126.

24. *Daily Telegraph*, 1 May 1996.

25. Dawkins, *The Selfish Gene*, p. 201.

26. Antony Flew, *There is a God*, HarperCollins Publishers, p. 80.

27. Richard Dawkins, *The Greatest Show on Earth*, Bantam Books, p. 6.

28. Ibid. p. 3.

29. Ibid. p. 8.

30. Ibid. p. 430.

31. Ibid. p. 434.

32. Ibid. p. 9.

33. Ibid. p. 13.

34. Ibid. p. 10.

35. *Newsnight Review*, BBC 1, 9 September 2009.

36. Dawkins, *The Greatest Show on Earth*, p. 6.

37. Ibid. p. 6.

38. Ibid. p. 9.

39.  www.dissentfromdarwin.org.

40.  Dawkins, *The Greatest Show on Earth*, p. 9.

41.  Ibid. p. 8.

42.  Ibid. p. 18.

43.  Dawkins, *The Blind Watchmaker*, pp. 287–8.

44.  David Robertson, *The Dawkins Letters*, Christian Focus Publications, p. 30.

45.  See Victor Steger, *God the Failed Hypothesis*, Prometheus Books, p. 28, ref. 1.

46.  Francis Collins, *The Language of God*, Free Press, p. 6.

47.  Richard Dawkins, *A Devil's Chaplain*, Houghton Mifflin, p. 149.

## 3. Morality: rights and wrongs

1.   Dawkins, *The God Delusion*, p. 2.

2.   *Heart of the Matter*, BBC Television, 29 September 1996.

3.   Dawkins, *The Selfish Gene*, p. 2.

4.   Ibid. pp. 200–201.

5.   Dawkins, *The God Delusion*, p. 221.

6.   Kathleen Jones, *Challenging Richard Dawkins*, Canterbury Press, p. 40.

7.   See *The God Delusion*, pp. 237–50.

8.   Dawkins, *The God Delusion*, p. 248.

9.   Ibid. p. 237.

10.  Ibid. p. 238.

11.  Ibid.

12.  Ibid.

13.  Ibid. pp. 270–71.

14.  Ibid. p. 262.

15. John C. Lennox, *God's Undertaker*, Lion Hudson.

16. Alabama debate.

17. Dawkins, *A Devil's Chaplain*, p. 34.

18. Dawkins, *The God Delusion*, p. 262.

19. Ibid. p. 271.

20. Jones, *Challenging Richard Dawkins*, p. 143.

21. Ibid. p. 142.

22. *Daily Telegraph*, 31 August 1992.

23. C. S. Lewis, *Miracles*, Collins, p. 122.

24. Cited by Phillip E. Johnson, *Darwin on Trial*, Monarch Publications, p. 114.

25. Edgar Andrews, *Who Made God?*, EP Books, p. 270.

26. J. L. Mackie, *The Miracle of Theism*, Clarendon, p. 116.

27. Gary E. Gilley with Jay Wegter, *This Little Church had None*, EP Books, p. 178.

28. Dawkins, *The God Delusion*, p. 232.

29. Scott Hahn and Benjamin Wiker, *Answering the New Atheism*, Emmaus Road Publishing, p. 97.

30. Richard Dawkins, *River out of Eden*, Basic Books, p. 133.

31. Francis Collins, *The Language of God*, Free Press, p. 218.

## 4. Religion: the root of all evil?

1. Alister McGrath, *The Dawkins Delusion*, SPCK, p. xi.

2. Dawkins, *The God Delusion*, p. 249.

3. *Omni 12* (4), January 1990.

4. Statement to Freedom from Religion Foundation, Madison, Wisconsin, September 2001.

5. Christopher Hitchens, *God is not Great*, Atlantic Books, p. 13.

6. Dawkins, *The God Delusion*, pp. 1–2.

7. See Dawkins, *The God Delusion*, p. 259.

8. Cited in McGrath, *The Dawkins Delusion*, p. 27.

9. See Dawkins, *The God Delusion*, p. 249.

10. Nicolai Lenin, *Selected Works*, vol. XL, Lawrence and Wishart Ltd, pp. 675–6.

11. Speech by Adolf Hitler, 12 April 1922.

12. Adolf Hitler, *Table Talk*, 1941.

13. Dawkins, *The God Delusion*, p. 278.

14. Dinesh D'Souza, *What's so Great about Christianity?*, Regnery Publishing, p. 215.

15. Alister McGrath, *The Twilight of Atheism*, Doubleday, p. 230.

16. Michael Shermer, *How we Believe: Science, Skepticism and the Search for God*, Freeman, p. 71.

17. Dawkins, *The God Delusion*, p. 253.

18. Ibid. p. 237.

19. Ibid. p. 264.

## 5. God: necessary or non-existent?

1. Dawkins, *The God Delusion*, p. 31.

2. Ibid. p. 27.

3. Ibid. p. 31.

4. Collins, *The Language of God*, p. 164.

5. Dawkins, *The God Delusion*, p. 157.

6. Thomas Nagel, 'The Fear of Religion', in *The New Republic*, 23 October 2006.

7. Dawkins, *The God Delusion*, p. 50

8. Collins, *The Language of God*, p. 30.

9.   Stephen J. Gould, 'Impeaching a Self-appointed Judge', *Scientific American 267*; see pp. 118–21.

10.  C. S. Lewis, *The Weight of Glory and Other Addresses*, HarperCollins, p. 140.

11.  Dawkins, *The God Delusion*, p. 134.

12.  Andrews. *Who Made God?*, p. 23.

13.  Keith Ward, *God, Chance and Necessity*, Oneworld Publications, p. 109.

14.  Stephen J. Gould, *Wonderful Life: The Burgess Shale and the Nature of History*, W. W. Norton & Co., p. 291.

15.  Ward, *God, Chance and Necessity*, p. 115.

16.  Collins, *The Language of God*, p. 21.

17.  Ibid. p. 93.

## 6. The Bible: the book that speaks for itself

1.   Dawkins, *The God Delusion*, p. 341.

2.   Ibid. p. 343.

3.   F. F. Bruce, *Second Thoughts on the Dead Sea Scrolls*, Paternoster Press, pp. 61–2.

4.   Dawkins, *The God Delusion*, p. 93.

5.   Ibid. p. 97.

6.   William Ramsay, *The Bearing of Recent Discovery on the Trustworthiness of the New Testament*, Hodder and Stoughton, p. 222.

7.   Cited by Dave Hunt, *Defense of the Faith*, Harvest House Publishers, p. 144.

8.   Donald Wiseman, 'Digging for Truth', *Viewpoint No. 31*, Inter Schools Christian Fellowship.

9. Frederic G. Kenyon, *The Bible and Archaeology*, Harper & Row, p. 288.

10. Dawkins, *The God Delusion*, p. 93.

11. Ibid.

12. Ibid.

13. Ibid. p. 96.

14. Ibid. p. 257.

15. Ibid. p. 94.

16. Ibid. p. 237.

17. Ibid. p. 238.

18. Terry Eagleton, *London Review of Books*, 19 October 2006.

19. Dawkins, *The God Delusion*, p. 344.

20. John Frame, *Apologetics to the Glory of God*, P & R Publishing, p. 121.

21. J. I. Packer, *God Has Spoken*, Hodder and Stoughton, p. 106.

## 7. Christianity: evidence and effects

1. Dawkins, *The God Delusion*, p. 37.

2. Ibid.

3. Ibid.

4. Ibid.

5. *The Guardian*, 11 October 2001.

6. Hitchens, *God is not Great*, p. 74.

7. Cited by James M. Byrne, *Religion and the Enlightenment: From Descartes to Kant*, John Knox Press.

8. Marianna Krejci-Papa, 2005. 'Taking On Dawkins' God: An interview with Alister McGrath.' *Science & Theology News*, 25 April 2005.

9. Nagel, *The New Republic*, 23 October 2006.

10. Eagleton, *London Review of Books*, 19 October 2006.

## 8. Jesus: the man for all reasons

1. Dawkins, *The God Delusion*, p. 97.

2. See *The God Delusion*, pp. 95–6.

3. *Saturday Evening Post*, 26 October 1929.

4. Dawkins, *The God Delusion*, p. 92.

5. See John Blanchard, *Meet the Real Jesus*, EP Books, pp. 151–81.

6. Dawkins, *The God Delusion*, p. 250.

7. Ibid. p. 251.

8. Ibid.

9. Ibid. p. 253.

10. Ibid.

11. John R. W. Stott, *The Cross of Christ*, Inter Varsity Press, pp. 326–7.

12. Dawkins, *The God Delusion*, p. 253

13. Ibid.

14. Ibid. p. 59.

15. *The Independent*, 4 December 2006.

16. Alabama debate.

17. Dawkins, *The God Delusion*, p. 59.

18. See pp. 578–84; *Meet the Real Jesus*, EP Books, pp. 117–50; *Jesus: Dead or Alive?*, EP Books.

19. A. Rendle Short, *Why Believe?*, Inter-Varsity Press, p. 51.

20. J. N. D. Anderson, *Jesus Christ: The Witness of History*, Inter Varsity Press, p. 146.

21. E. G. Robinson, *Christian Theology*, E. R. Andrews.

22. D. James Kennedy, *The Gates of Hell shall not Prevail*, Thomas Nelson Publishers, p. 21.

23. *The Times*, 27 December 2008.

24. Cited by Michael Green, *Man Alive!*, Inter Varsity Press, p. 54.

25. Andrew Wilson, *Deluded by Dawkins?*, Kingsway Publications, p. 82.

## 9. Faith: beyond the facts

1. Dawkins, *The Selfish Gene*, p. 118.

2. Dawkins, *A Devil's Chaplain*, p. 117.

3. Dawkins, *The Selfish Gene* (second edition), p. 330.

4. See, e.g., Dawkins, *The God Delusion*, pp. 51ff.

5. Jones, *Challenging Richard Dawkins*, p. 49.

6. Alister McGrath, *Dawkins' God*, Blackwell Publishing, p. 102.

7. Stephen Hawking, *A Brief History of Time*, Bantam Books, pp. 140–41.

8. Keith Ward, *Why There Almost Certainly is a God*, Lion Publishing, p. 81.

9. Bertrand Russell, *Autobiography*, George Allen & Unwin, p. 303.

10. Stuart Olyott, *The Gospel as it Really is*, EP Books, p. 9.

11. Brian Edwards, *Through Many Dangers*, EP Books, p. 24.